GENOA TRAVEL GUIDE 2024

Exciting Things To Do In Genoa

Bonita Green

Table of content

Introduction

Welcome to Genoa

Welcome to Genoa, a captivating city coastline of the Ligurian Sea in northern Italy. As you step foot into this vibrant metropolis, you'll find yourself immersed in a rich tapestry of history, culture, and culinary delights. From its ancient maritime heritage to its bustling contemporary atmosphere,

Genoa offers a unique blend of old-world charm and modern sophistication.

A Glimpse into Genoa's Past:
Genoa boasts a storied past that dates back over two millennia. Once a powerful maritime republic, it flourished as a key trading hub during the Middle Ages, establishing commercial networks that stretched across the Mediterranean and beyond. The city's wealth and influence are evident in its grand palaces, ornate churches, and labyrinthine alleyways, each bearing witness to centuries of prosperity and prestige.

Exploring Genoa's Architectural Marvels:
One of the highlights of any visit to Genoa is its remarkable architecture. Wander through the narrow streets of the historic center and

marvel at the elegant facades of medieval palaces and Renaissance mansions. Admire the intricate detailing of buildings such as the Palazzo Ducale, once the seat of the city's rulers, and the Palazzi dei Rolli, a collection of sumptuous residences recognized as a UNESCO World Heritage site. At every turn, you'll encounter reminders of Genoa's illustrious past and its enduring architectural legacy.

The Allure of Genoa's Waterfront:

No visit to Genoa would be complete without a stroll along its picturesque waterfront. The Old Port, once the heart of the city's maritime activities, has been transformed into a vibrant leisure destination, brimming with cafes, restaurants, and cultural attractions. Explore the exhibits at the Galata Maritime Museum, housed within a striking modern structure overlooking the harbor, or simply relax and soak in the views of the sparkling sea.

Embracing Genoa's Cultural Diversity:

Genoa's cultural landscape is as diverse as its history, with influences ranging from Mediterranean to Alpine and beyond. The city's vibrant street life reflects this rich tapestry of traditions, with colorful markets, lively festivals, and bustling piazzas providing a glimpse into everyday life. Discover the works of renowned artists at museums such as the Palazzo Bianco and the Palazzo Rosso, or explore the contemporary art scene in the city's burgeoning gallery district.

Culinary Delights of the Ligurian Coast:

No visit to Genoa would be complete without indulging in its culinary delights. From fragrant pesto to freshly caught seafood, the flavors of Ligurian cuisine are sure to tantalize your taste buds. Sample traditional dishes at local trattorias and osterias, or embark on a culinary adventure through the city's bustling markets, where vendors proudly display their bountiful harvest of fruits, vegetables, and artisanal products.

Why Visit Genoa in 2024?

In the year 2024, Genoa beckons travelers with an irresistible allure, offering a myriad of compelling reasons to explore this enchanting city on the Italian Riviera. From its rich history and cultural vibrancy to its stunning natural beauty and culinary delights, Genoa stands as a must-visit destination for discerning travelers seeking an authentic and unforgettable experience.

Renewed Vibrancy and Energy:

As the world emerges from the challenges of recent years, Genoa is experiencing a renaissance, infused with a renewed sense of vibrancy and energy. The city's streets are alive with activity, as locals and visitors alike come together to celebrate life, culture, and community. From vibrant festivals and cultural events to lively markets and bustling piazzas, there's an unmistakable sense of optimism and joie de vivre permeating the air.

Cultural Capital of Liguria:

Genoa has long been celebrated as the cultural capital of Liguria, boasting a wealth of artistic, architectural, and historical treasures waiting to be discovered. In 2024, the city continues to captivate with its rich heritage, offering travelers a glimpse into its illustrious past through its magnificent palaces, churches, and museums. Explore the grandeur of the Palazzo Ducale, delve into the city's maritime history at the Galata Maritime Museum, or wander through the atmospheric alleyways of the historic center, where echoes of centuries past linger at every turn.

Gateway to the Italian Riviera:
Situated along the stunning coastline of the Italian Riviera, Genoa serves as the perfect gateway to a region of unparalleled beauty. In 2024, travelers can explore the rugged cliffs and azure waters of the Ligurian Sea, discovering hidden coves, charming fishing villages, and picturesque seaside towns along the way. From the colorful cliffside villages of Cinque Terre to the exclusive

resorts of Portofino and Santa Margherita Ligure, the possibilities for exploration are endless.

Culinary Delights and Gastronomic Adventures:

No visit to Genoa would be complete without indulging in its culinary delights, and 2024 is no exception. The city's gastronomic scene is a testament to its rich maritime heritage, with fresh seafood, fragrant herbs, and locally sourced ingredients taking center stage on every menu. Savor the flavors of Ligurian cuisine at traditional trattorias and waterfront restaurants, sample freshly caught fish at the bustling Mercato Orientale, or learn the art of pesto-making from local chefs during a hands-on cooking class.

Sustainable Tourism and Responsible Travel:

In an era of increasing awareness and concern for the environment, Genoa is leading the way in sustainable tourism and responsible travel practices. In 2024, travelers can explore the city with peace of mind, knowing that efforts are being made to preserve its natural beauty and cultural heritage for future generations. From eco-friendly accommodations and green transportation options to initiatives aimed at reducing waste and promoting conservation, Genoa is committed to ensuring that visitors can enjoy its treasures in a way that is both responsible and respectful.

Conclusion:

In 2024, Genoa invites travelers to embark on a journey of discovery, offering a compelling blend of history, culture, and natural beauty that promises to captivate the imagination and nourish the soul. Whether you're drawn to its rich heritage, its stunning coastline, or its delectable cuisine, Genoa is sure to leave an indelible impression, inviting you to return again and again to uncover its many treasures. So come, explore, and experience the magic of Genoa in 2024 – a city that continues to inspire, delight, and enchant all who visit.

Getting Around Genoa

Navigating the streets of Genoa is a delightful adventure that offers travelers a chance to immerse themselves in the city's unique atmosphere and vibrant energy. From its historic center filled with narrow alleyways and charming piazzas to its modern waterfront promenades, Genoa offers a variety of transportation options to suit every traveler's needs. In this comprehensive guide to getting around Genoa, we'll explore the various modes of transportation available, as well as provide tips and recommendations for making the most of your journey through this enchanting city.

Public Transportation:

Genoa boasts an extensive public transportation network that makes it easy to explore the city and its surrounding areas. The backbone of the system is the metro, which consists of both underground and above-ground lines that connect key neighborhoods and attractions. Additionally, buses and trams crisscross the city, providing convenient access to destinations not served by the metro. Travelers can purchase tickets and passes at metro stations, newsstands, and tobacco shops, with options available for single rides, day passes, and multi-day passes for unlimited travel.

Walking and Cycling:

One of the best ways to experience Genoa is on foot, allowing travelers to meander through its historic streets and soak in the sights, sounds, and smells of the city. The historic center, with its pedestrian-friendly alleyways and bustling squares, is particularly well-suited for walking, offering endless opportunities for exploration and discovery. For those looking to cover more ground, cycling is also a popular option, with bike rental shops scattered throughout the city. Genoa's network of bike lanes and waterfront promenades provide scenic routes for cyclists of all levels, making it easy to pedal your way from one attraction to the next.

Taxis and Ride-Sharing Services:

Taxis are readily available in Genoa, offering a convenient and comfortable way to get around the city, especially for travelers with limited mobility or heavy luggage. Taxis can be hailed on the street or found at designated taxi stands located throughout the city center and at major transportation hubs. Alternatively, ride-sharing services such as Uber and Lyft operate in Genoa, providing another option for travelers seeking on-demand transportation at the touch of a button.

Funiculars and Elevators:

Given Genoa's hilly terrain, funiculars and elevators play a crucial role in connecting different parts of the city and providing access to its scenic viewpoints. The city is home to several funicular railways, including the Zecca-Righi Funicular, which ascends to the panoramic Righi Hill, offering sweeping views of the city below. Additionally, a network of elevators and escalators known as "ascensori pubblici" provides vertical transportation between different levels of the city, making it easier for travelers to navigate its steep streets and staircases.

Conclusion:

Getting around Genoa is a breeze, thanks to its efficient public transportation system, pedestrian-friendly streets, and convenient access to taxis and ride-sharing services. Whether you choose to explore on foot, by bike, or using public transit, you'll find that Genoa is a city best experienced at a leisurely pace, allowing you to savor every moment and uncover its hidden gems along the way. So lace up your walking shoes, hop on a bike, or simply sit back and enjoy the ride – adventure awaits around every corner in the charming city of Genoa.

Chapter One: Exploring Genoa's Historical Treasures

The Old Port and Maritime Museum

Introduction:

The Old Port of Genoa, known locally as Porto Antico, stands as a testament to the city's rich maritime heritage and storied past as a prominent maritime republic. Situated at the heart of Genoa's waterfront, the Old Port has undergone a remarkable transformation in recent years, evolving from a bustling commercial harbor into a vibrant leisure and cultural hub. At its center lies the

Galata Maritime Museum, a captivating institution dedicated to preserving and showcasing the city's seafaring history.

History of the Old Port:

The history of the Old Port dates back over 2,000 years, making it one of the oldest ports in Europe. Originally established by the ancient Romans as a vital trading post, the port flourished during the Middle Ages, serving as a crucial hub for maritime commerce and exploration. Genoa's maritime prowess reached its zenith during the Renaissance, when the city emerged as a dominant force in Mediterranean trade, establishing colonies and trading outposts across the region.

Transformation and Revitalization:

In the late 20th century, the Old Port underwent a significant transformation, as the decline of traditional maritime industries prompted city leaders to re-imagine its role and potential. The result was a comprehensive redevelopment project that sought to revitalize the waterfront and create a dynamic urban space that would attract visitors and residents alike. Today, the Old Port is a thriving destination that seamlessly blends historic charm with modern amenities, offering a diverse array of attractions, restaurants, shops, and entertainment venues.

Highlights of the Old Port:
- Galata Maritime Museum: Housed within a striking modern building designed by architect Renzo Piano, the Galata Maritime Museum is a treasure trove of maritime artifacts, models, and interactive exhibits. Visitors can explore the museum's extensive collection, which spans centuries of

maritime history and encompasses everything from ancient navigational instruments to full-scale replicas of historic ships.

- Bigo Panoramic Lift: Offering panoramic views of the city and the surrounding coastline, the Bigo Panoramic Lift is a must-visit attraction for anyone exploring the Old Port. Originally a crane used for loading and unloading cargo ships, the Bigo has been transformed into an observation deck that rises 40 meters above the harbor, providing visitors with breathtaking vistas of Genoa's skyline and the Ligurian Sea.

- Aquarium of Genoa: Situated adjacent to the Galata Maritime Museum, the Aquarium of Genoa is one of the largest and most prestigious aquariums in Europe. Home to over 15,000 aquatic creatures representing

400 species, the aquarium offers visitors a fascinating journey through the world's oceans, from the depths of the abyss to the coral reefs of the tropics. Highlights include a walk-through shark tank, a dolphin and sea lion show, and interactive exhibits that educate and inspire visitors of all ages.

Conclusion:

The Old Port of Genoa stands as a vibrant testament to the city's maritime legacy, offering visitors a captivating blend of history, culture, and entertainment. Whether you're exploring the exhibits at the Galata Maritime Museum, marveling at the panoramic views from the Bigo Panoramic Lift, or discovering the wonders of the deep at the Aquarium of Genoa, the Old Port invites you to embark on a journey of discovery and exploration that will leave you with a deeper appreciation for Genoa's rich maritime heritage.

Palazzo Ducale and the Doge's Palace

Introduction:

Palazzo Ducale, also known as the Doge's Palace, is a magnificent architectural gem that serves as a symbol of Genoa's illustrious past and cultural heritage. Situated in the heart of the historic center, this grand Renaissance palace has played a central role in the city's political, social, and artistic life for centuries. Today, it stands as a testament to Genoa's rich history and serves as a cultural hub, hosting exhibitions, events, and performances that celebrate the city's legacy.

History of Palazzo Ducale:

Originally built in the 13th century as the residence of the Doge, or chief magistrate, Palazzo Ducale underwent several expansions and renovations over the centuries, reflecting the changing tastes and aspirations of Genoa's ruling elite. The palace served as the seat of government for the Republic of Genoa, housing the offices of the Doge, the Council of Elders, and other administrative bodies responsible for governing the city-state. It also served as a venue for diplomatic meetings, banquets, and celebrations, showcasing the wealth and power of the Genoese Republic to visitors from near and far.

Architectural Splendor:

The architectural splendor of Palazzo Ducale is evident in its majestic facades, elegant courtyards, and sumptuously decorated interiors. The palace boasts a blend of architectural styles, including Gothic, Renaissance, and Baroque elements, reflecting the tastes and influences of the different periods in which it was constructed and renovated. Visitors can admire the intricate detailing of the facade, with its soaring arches, ornate balconies, and sculpted reliefs, or explore the richly decorated halls and chambers within, which showcase masterpieces of Genoese art and craftsmanship.

Highlights of Palazzo Ducale:
- The Grand Council Chamber: One of the most impressive rooms in Palazzo Ducale is the Grand Council Chamber, a vast hall adorned with frescoes depicting scenes

from Genoa's history, mythology, and civic life. This majestic space served as the meeting place for the city's ruling council, where decisions of state were debated and enacted. Visitors can marvel at the grandeur of the chamber and imagine the echoes of centuries past that linger within its walls.

- The Doge's Apartments: The private quarters of the Doge offer a glimpse into the opulent lifestyle of Genoa's ruling elite. Lavishly decorated with stucco, marble, and gilt, these rooms reflect the wealth and power of the Doge, who presided over the city as both a political leader and a symbol of authority. Visitors can wander through the Doge's private chambers, admiring the rich furnishings and exquisite artwork that adorned his residence.

- The Courtyard and Loggia: The courtyard of Palazzo Ducale is a tranquil oasis in the heart of the city, surrounded by arcaded galleries and adorned with statues, fountains, and lush greenery. The Loggia degli Ambasciatori, or Ambassador's Loggia, overlooks the courtyard and provides panoramic views of the city and harbor below. This airy terrace was used for receiving foreign dignitaries and hosting diplomatic events, and today it serves as a scenic spot for visitors to pause and reflect on the beauty and history of Palazzo Ducale.

Conclusion:

Palazzo Ducale and the Doge's Palace stand as enduring symbols of Genoa's rich cultural heritage and architectural legacy. From its majestic facades and opulent interiors to its historic significance as a seat of power and governance, the palace offers visitors a fascinating glimpse into the grandeur and splendor of Genoa's golden age. Whether you're marveling at the frescoes in the Grand Council Chamber, exploring the Doge's private apartments, or simply soaking in the atmosphere of the courtyard, a visit to Palazzo Ducale is sure to leave you with a deeper appreciation for the history and culture of this captivating city.

Via Garibaldi and the Rolli Palaces

Introduction:

Via Garibaldi, formerly known as Strada Nuova, is a historic street in the heart of Genoa's city center, renowned for its stunning collection of Renaissance palaces known as the Rolli Palaces. These palaces were once the residences of Genoa's noble families and were recognized by UNESCO as a World Heritage Site in 2006 for their outstanding architectural and artistic value. Today, Via Garibaldi and the Rolli Palaces offer visitors a glimpse into the opulent lifestyle and artistic splendor of Genoa's golden age.

History of Via Garibaldi and the Rolli Palaces:

Constructed in the late 16th century, Via Garibaldi was originally designed as a grand thoroughfare connecting the city's commercial and residential districts. It quickly became the preferred address for Genoa's wealthiest families, who commissioned renowned architects and artists to build elaborate palaces that would showcase their wealth and status. The result was a stunning ensemble of palaces that exemplified the principles of Renaissance architecture and urban planning, with harmonious proportions, elegant facades, and ornate interiors that reflected the taste and sophistication of the city's elite.

Exploring the Rolli Palaces:

The Rolli Palaces line both sides of Via Garibaldi, forming an impressive architectural ensemble that spans several blocks. Each palace is unique in its design and decoration, reflecting the individual tastes and preferences of its original occupants. Visitors can marvel at the richly decorated facades, adorned with sculpted reliefs, intricate stonework, and ornamental details that testify to the skill and craftsmanship of the artisans who created them. Many of the palaces are open to the public, allowing visitors to explore their sumptuous interiors, which feature frescoes, stucco work, and fine furnishings that evoke the opulence of Renaissance Genoa.

Highlights of Via Garibaldi and the Rolli Palaces:

- Palazzo Rosso: One of the most famous palaces on Via Garibaldi, Palazzo Rosso is home to a superb collection of paintings, sculptures, and decorative arts from the 17th and 18th centuries. Highlights include works by artists such as Van Dyck, Rubens, and Veronese, as well as a series of lavishly decorated rooms that provide insight into the daily life and social customs of Genoa's aristocracy.

- Palazzo Bianco: Adjacent to Palazzo Rosso, Palazzo Bianco is another magnificent palace that houses an impressive collection of art and antiquities. Visitors can admire works by Italian and

European masters, including Caravaggio, Guido Reni, and Giovanni Battista Tiepolo, as well as exquisite examples of decorative arts such as furniture, ceramics, and textiles.

- Palazzo Doria Tursi: Located at the eastern end of Via Garibaldi, Palazzo Doria Tursi is home to the Genoa City Hall and the Municipal Art Gallery. The palace's richly decorated rooms and halls are adorned with paintings, sculptures, and historic artifacts that trace the history of the city and its illustrious patrons, including the powerful Doria and Tursi families.

Conclusion:
Via Garibaldi and the Rolli Palaces offer visitors a fascinating journey through the history, art, and architecture of Renaissance Genoa. Whether you're marveling at the opulent facades of the palaces, exploring

their sumptuous interiors, or admiring the masterpieces of art and antiquities they contain, a stroll along Via Garibaldi is sure to transport you back in time to the golden age of the Republic of Genoa. Soak in the splendor of these historic treasures and discover the timeless beauty of Genoa's cultural heritage along this iconic street.

Chapter Two: Immersing in Genoa's Cultural Delights

Genoa's Vibrant Street Art Scene

Introduction:

Genoa's streets are alive with creativity, color, and expression, thanks to its vibrant street art scene. From sprawling murals adorning building facades to hidden gems tucked away in narrow alleyways, the city serves as a canvas for local and international artists to showcase their talents and share their messages with the world. In this chapter, we'll delve into the dynamic world of Genoa's street art, exploring its origins, evolution, and the diverse array of artworks that adorn its urban landscape.

Origins of Genoa's Street Art Scene:

The roots of Genoa's street art scene can be traced back to the late 20th century, when a wave of artistic experimentation and cultural activism swept through the city's neighborhoods. Inspired by global movements such as hip-hop culture and graffiti art, local artists began to transform the city's blank walls and neglected spaces into vibrant works of art, using spray paint, stencils, and other unconventional materials to express themselves and engage with their communities.

Evolution of Street Art in Genoa:

Over the years, Genoa's street art scene has evolved and diversified, encompassing a wide range of styles, techniques, and themes. While graffiti and murals remain central to the movement, artists have increasingly embraced other forms of expression, including stencil art, wheatpaste posters, and guerrilla installations. The result is a dynamic and eclectic landscape that reflects the city's cultural diversity, social issues, and artistic experimentation.

Exploring Genoa's Street Art:

One of the best ways to experience Genoa's street art scene is to take a self-guided walking tour of the city, exploring its neighborhoods and seeking out hidden gems tucked away in unexpected corners. Start your journey in the historic center, where colorful murals and graffiti tags adorn the walls of centuries-old buildings, juxtaposing the city's ancient architecture with contemporary artistic expression.

Highlights of Genoa's Street Art Scene:

- Via San Bernardo: This narrow street in the heart of the historic center is a hotspot for street art, with its walls covered in vibrant murals and graffiti tags. Explore the alleyways and side streets off Via San Bernardo to discover hidden artworks and unexpected surprises around every corner.

- Sant'Agostino District: Located just outside the historic center, the Sant'Agostino district is home to a thriving street art community, with its industrial buildings and abandoned warehouses providing a blank canvas for artists to work their magic. Take a stroll through the neighborhood to admire the large-scale murals and installations that adorn its streets, or join a guided tour to learn more about the artists and their creative process.

- Murales di Nervi: For a glimpse into the world of contemporary street art, head to the seaside district of Nervi, where a series of colorful murals decorate the walls along the waterfront promenade. Created by local and international artists, these striking artworks celebrate the beauty of nature, the power of community, and the spirit of creativity that defines Genoa's street art scene.

Conclusion:

Genoa's street art scene is a vibrant reflection of the city's creativity, diversity, and vitality. Whether you're exploring the historic center, venturing into the neighborhoods, or strolling along the waterfront, you'll find yourself surrounded by a kaleidoscope of colors, shapes, and stories that capture the essence of contemporary Genoa. Soak in the sights, embrace the energy, and immerse yourself in the dynamic world of street art as you discover the artistic treasures hidden within the streets of this captivating city.

Teatro Carlo Felice and Genoa's Opera Tradition

Introduction:

Teatro Carlo Felice stands as a beacon of cultural excellence in the heart of Genoa, serving as the city's premier venue for opera, ballet, and classical music performances. Named in honor of King Charles Felix of Sardinia, who laid the foundation stone for the theater in 1826, Teatro Carlo Felice has played a central role in Genoa's artistic and social life for nearly two centuries. In this chapter, we'll explore the history of the theater, its architectural splendor, and the enduring legacy of Genoa's opera tradition.

History of Teatro Carlo Felice:

Teatro Carlo Felice has a storied history that dates back to the early 19th century, when Genoa's aristocracy sought to establish a grand opera house that would rival those of other European cities. Designed by architect Carlo Barabino, the theater was built in the neoclassical style, with a magnificent facade adorned with Corinthian columns, sculpted reliefs, and a grand portico. It quickly became the cultural centerpiece of Genoa, attracting world-renowned artists and musicians to perform on its stage and delighting audiences with spectacular productions of opera, ballet, and symphonic music.

Renovation and Restoration:
Over the years, Teatro Carlo Felice has undergone several renovations and restorations to ensure its continued relevance and vitality. In the aftermath of

World War II, the theater suffered extensive damage during bombing raids, prompting a major reconstruction effort that restored its grandeur and beauty. More recently, in the early 21st century, the theater underwent a comprehensive renovation that modernized its facilities, improved its acoustics, and enhanced the overall visitor experience, while preserving its historic charm and architectural integrity.

Opera Tradition in Genoa:

Genoa has a long-standing tradition of opera that dates back centuries, with the city's aristocracy and merchant elite serving as patrons and supporters of the arts. Teatro Carlo Felice has been at the center of this tradition, hosting world-class opera productions that showcase the talents of both local and international artists. From beloved classics by composers such as Verdi, Puccini, and Rossini to contemporary works by emerging talents, the theater's repertoire spans the gamut of operatic genres and styles, offering something for every taste and preference.

Highlights of Teatro Carlo Felice:

- Opera Performances: The highlight of any visit to Teatro Carlo Felice is undoubtedly attending a live opera performance. Whether you're a seasoned opera aficionado or a newcomer to the art form, the theater's world-class productions, lavish sets, and stellar performances are sure to leave you spellbound. From tragic love stories to comic operas, the theater's diverse repertoire ensures that there's always something new and exciting to experience.

- Ballet and Dance: In addition to opera, Teatro Carlo Felice also hosts performances by leading ballet companies and contemporary dance troupes from around the world. From classic ballets such as Swan Lake and The Nutcracker to innovative contemporary works by cutting-edge choreographers, the theater's dance program offers a captivating blend of tradition and innovation that delights audiences of all ages.

- Concerts and Recitals: Throughout the year, Teatro Carlo Felice presents a diverse array of concerts and recitals featuring renowned soloists, chamber ensembles, and orchestras. From symphonic masterpieces to intimate chamber music, these performances showcase the exceptional talent and artistry of the musicians who grace the theater's stage, providing audiences with unforgettable musical experiences that linger long after the final note has sounded.

Conclusion:

Teatro Carlo Felice stands as a cultural landmark and a testament to Genoa's enduring love affair with the arts. Whether you're attending a live opera performance, enjoying a ballet recital, or savoring a symphonic concert, the theater offers a wealth of artistic riches that inspire, entertain, and enrich the soul. Soak in the splendor of its neoclassical architecture, revel in the beauty of its performances, and immerse yourself in the timeless magic of Genoa's opera tradition at Teatro Carlo Felice.

Museums Galore: Exploring Art, History, and Science

Introduction:

Genoa boasts an impressive array of museums that cater to a wide range of interests, from art and history to science and technology. These cultural institutions offer visitors a chance to delve into the city's rich heritage, discover its artistic treasures, and explore the wonders of the natural world. In this chapter, we'll embark on a journey through Genoa's museums, highlighting their diverse collections, captivating exhibitions, and the unique insights they offer into the city's past, present, and future.

Art Museums:

Genoa is home to several world-class art museums that showcase masterpieces spanning centuries of artistic achievement. The Palazzo Bianco and Palazzo Rosso, located on Via Garibaldi, house superb collections of Italian and European art, including works by Caravaggio, Rubens, and Van Dyck. The Museo di Palazzo Reale, situated in the heart of the historic center, offers visitors a glimpse into the opulent lifestyle of Genoa's ruling elite, with its richly furnished rooms and galleries displaying paintings, sculptures, and decorative arts from the 16th to the 19th centuries.

History Museums:

For those interested in delving into Genoa's rich history, the city offers a wealth of museums and historic sites that shed light on its storied past. The Galata Maritime Museum, located in the Old Port, traces the city's maritime heritage through interactive exhibits, model ships, and artifacts from the age of exploration. The Museo di Storia e Cultura Ebraica, housed in a former synagogue in the historic Jewish quarter, explores the history and culture of Genoa's Jewish community through displays of religious objects, documents, and photographs.

Science Museums:

Genoa's museums also offer fascinating insights into the world of science and technology. The Museo di Storia Naturale, located in the Palazzo Doria Tursi, features exhibits on geology, paleontology, and biodiversity, showcasing specimens from around the world and highlighting the region's natural heritage. The Museo Galileo, housed in the former convent of San Matteo, explores the history of science and technology in Genoa and beyond, with displays of scientific instruments, astronomical artifacts, and interactive exhibits that bring the wonders of the universe to life.

Specialty Museums:

In addition to its art, history, and science museums, Genoa is home to several specialty museums that cater to more specific interests. The Museo del Tesoro di San Lorenzo, located in the crypt of the Cathedral of San Lorenzo, showcases religious artifacts, reliquaries, and liturgical objects dating back to the Middle Ages. The Museo della Lanterna, housed in Genoa's iconic lighthouse, offers visitors a chance to learn about the history and technology of maritime navigation, with exhibits on lighthouse design, shipwrecks, and maritime rescue operations.

Conclusion:

Genoa's museums offer a rich tapestry of experiences that celebrate the city's cultural heritage, artistic achievements, and scientific discoveries. Whether you're exploring the masterpieces of the Palazzo Bianco, delving into the history of the Galata Maritime Museum, or marveling at the wonders of the Museo di Storia Naturale, each museum offers a unique window into the soul of Genoa and invites visitors to embark on a journey of discovery and exploration that will leave them with a deeper appreciation for the city and its treasures.

Chapter Three: Savory Delights of Genoa's Gastronomy

The Flavors of Ligurian Cuisine: Pesto and Focaccia

Introduction:

Ligurian cuisine is a celebration of fresh, simple ingredients and bold flavors, inspired by the region's abundant coastline, fertile valleys, and sun-drenched hillsides. At the heart of Ligurian gastronomy are two iconic dishes that have become synonymous with the region: pesto and focaccia. In this chapter, we'll explore the origins of these culinary delights, their unique ingredients and preparation methods, and where to find the best examples in Genoa.

Pesto: A Taste of Summer:

Pesto, the quintessential Ligurian sauce, is a vibrant blend of fresh basil, pine nuts, garlic, Parmesan cheese, and extra virgin olive oil. Traditionally made by hand using a mortar and pestle, pesto captures the essence of summer in Liguria, with its bright green color and fragrant aroma evoking the flavors of the Mediterranean. Genoa, the birthplace of pesto, takes pride in its culinary heritage, with countless trattorias and restaurants serving up this beloved sauce in a variety of dishes, from pasta and risotto to sandwiches and salads.

Focaccia: The Bread of Liguria:

Focaccia, a type of flatbread made from yeast dough, olive oil, and sea salt, is another staple of Ligurian cuisine. Light and airy, with a crisp crust and a tender crumb, focaccia is a versatile canvas for a wide range of toppings and flavors. In Genoa, focaccia is often enjoyed plain or with a drizzle of olive oil and a sprinkle of rosemary or sea salt, but it can also be filled with ingredients such as cheese, olives, or onions to create a more substantial meal. Whether enjoyed as a snack, a side dish, or a light meal, focaccia is a beloved symbol of Ligurian culinary tradition.

Where to Find the Best Pesto and Focaccia in Genoa:

- Antica Osteria di Vico Palla: This charming trattoria, located in the heart of the historic center, is renowned for its traditional Ligurian cuisine, including homemade pesto served with trofie pasta, a local specialty.

- Panificio Girardengo: For some of the best focaccia in Genoa, head to this historic bakery in the Carignano district, where you can sample a variety of freshly baked focaccia topped with classic ingredients like olives, onions, and cherry tomatoes.

- Mercato Orientale: For a taste of authentic Ligurian flavors, visit this bustling market in the historic center, where you'll find vendors selling fresh basil, pine nuts, and other ingredients for making pesto, as well as freshly baked focaccia and other local delicacies.

Conclusion:

Pesto and focaccia are more than just dishes in Ligurian cuisine; they are symbols of the region's rich culinary heritage and its close connection to the land and sea. Whether you're savoring a plate of trofie al pesto in a cozy trattoria or enjoying a slice of freshly baked focaccia from a local bakery, these iconic flavors of Genoa are sure to delight your taste buds and leave you craving more. So indulge in the flavors of Liguria, and discover why pesto and focaccia are beloved by locals and visitors alike in the charming city of Genoa.

Seafood Sensations: Where to Taste the Freshest Catches

Introduction:

As a coastal city, Genoa is renowned for its seafood delicacies, which are celebrated for their freshness, flavor, and variety. From succulent fish and shellfish to briny crustaceans and savory mollusks, the city's culinary scene is a paradise for seafood lovers. In this chapter, we'll embark on a gastronomic journey through Genoa's seafood hotspots, discovering where to find the freshest catches and savoring the flavors of the sea.

Ristorante Al Porto Antico:

Located in the historic Old Port of Genoa, Ristorante Al Porto Antico is a seafood lover's paradise, offering a menu that showcases the finest catches of the day. From grilled octopus and fried calamari to seafood risotto and linguine with clams, every dish is prepared with care and attention to detail, allowing the natural flavors of the ingredients to shine through. The restaurant's waterfront location offers stunning views of the harbor, making it the perfect spot to enjoy a leisurely meal while soaking in the sights and sounds of the sea.

Trattoria da Maria:

Nestled in the heart of the historic center, Trattoria da Maria is a beloved local institution known for its hearty seafood dishes and welcoming atmosphere. The menu features a variety of traditional Ligurian specialties, including stuffed squid, seafood stew, and grilled fish served with seasonal vegetables and potatoes. The restaurant's cozy interior and friendly service create a warm and inviting atmosphere that makes diners feel right at home, making it a favorite haunt for both locals and visitors alike.

Ristorante Boccadasse:

Perched on the picturesque waterfront of the Boccadasse neighborhood, Ristorante Boccadasse offers diners a taste of the sea in a stunning coastal setting. The restaurant's menu features an array of fresh seafood dishes, including grilled fish, seafood risotto, and mixed seafood platters, all prepared with the highest quality ingredients and expertly cooked to perfection. With its panoramic views of the Ligurian Sea and charming seaside ambiance, Ristorante Boccadasse is the ideal spot to enjoy a memorable meal while basking in the beauty of Genoa's coastline.

Conclusion:

Genoa's seafood scene is a testament to the city's close relationship with the sea and its rich maritime heritage. Whether you're dining at a waterfront restaurant in the Old Port, savoring traditional Ligurian fare in the historic center, or enjoying a meal with a view in the coastal neighborhood of Boccadasse, you'll find that the flavors of the sea are alive and well in every bite. So indulge in the freshest catches and savor the delights of Genoa's seafood sensations as you embark on a culinary adventure along the shores of the Ligurian Sea.

Traditional Cafés and Aperitivo Culture

Introduction:

Genoa's culinary scene is not only defined by its delicious seafood and iconic dishes but also by its vibrant café culture and cherished tradition of aperitivo. From historic cafés steeped in tradition to trendy bars serving up innovative cocktails, Genoa offers a diverse array of venues where locals and visitors alike can unwind, socialize, and savor the flavors of the city. In this chapter, we'll explore the world of traditional cafés and aperitivo culture in Genoa, delving into the history, rituals, and rituals of these beloved institutions.

Traditional Cafés:
Genoa's traditional cafés are more than just places to grab a cup of coffee; they are cultural institutions that have been serving as gathering spots for locals and

intellectuals for centuries. Café degli Specchi, located in the heart of the historic center, is one such establishment, with its elegant interior, ornate décor, and timeless charm evoking the grandeur of a bygone era. Here, patrons can enjoy a leisurely espresso or cappuccino while soaking in the ambiance of the café's historic surroundings, making it the perfect spot for a morning pick-me-up or an afternoon reprieve.

Aperitivo Culture:

Aperitivo is a cherished ritual in Genoa, where friends and colleagues gather after work to enjoy pre-dinner drinks and snacks in a convivial atmosphere. The tradition typically involves ordering a drink, such as an Aperol Spritz or a Negroni, which is accompanied by a selection of complimentary appetizers, ranging from olives and cheese to bruschetta and cured meats. Aperitivo hour is a time for relaxation, conversation, and camaraderie, with locals flocking to their favorite bars and cafés to unwind and socialize before heading home for the evening.

Where to Experience Traditional Cafés and Aperitivo in Genoa:

- Caffè Mangini: This historic café, located near the Piazza de Ferrari, has been serving up coffee and pastries since the 19th century. With its ornate décor, marble countertops, and elegant atmosphere, it's the perfect spot to enjoy a leisurely breakfast or afternoon espresso.

- Bar Boccaccio: For a taste of Genoa's aperitivo culture, head to Bar Boccaccio in the Carignano district, where you'll find a wide selection of cocktails, wines, and spirits, along with a generous spread of appetizers to enjoy with your drinks.

- Bar Nazionale: Situated in the heart of the historic center, Bar Nazionale is a popular spot for locals and visitors alike to enjoy aperitivo hour. With its cozy interior, friendly service, and mouthwatering selection of snacks, it's the perfect place to unwind after a day of sightseeing.

Conclusion:

Traditional cafés and aperitivo culture are integral parts of daily life in Genoa, offering locals and visitors alike a chance to unwind, socialize, and savor the flavors of the city.

Whether you're enjoying a cappuccino in a historic café, sipping cocktails at a trendy bar, or indulging in pre-dinner drinks and snacks with friends, the experience is sure to be memorable. So embrace the rituals of traditional cafés and aperitivo culture as you immerse yourself in the vibrant culinary scene of Genoa, and discover why these beloved traditions have stood the test of time in this captivating city.

Chapter Four: Venturing Beyond Genoa: Day Trips and Nearby Attractions

Portofino: A Gem of the Italian Riviera

Introduction:

The Italian Riviera, Portofino is a charming fishing village that has captivated visitors with its natural beauty, colorful buildings, and relaxed atmosphere for centuries. Famous for its stunning harbor, luxury boutiques, and celebrity sightings, Portofino exudes an air of timeless elegance and sophistication that continues to enchant travelers from around the world. In this chapter, we'll delve into the allure of Portofino, exploring its rich history, scenic landmarks, and the myriad of activities that await those who venture to this coastal paradise.

History and Heritage:

Portofino's history dates back to ancient times when it served as a Roman port and later as a strategic outpost for maritime trade and defense. Over the centuries, the village grew into a thriving fishing community, its colorful houses clinging to the rugged coastline like a cluster of jewels. Today, Portofino's historic center retains much of its old-world charm, with narrow cobblestone streets, quaint piazzas, and pastel-colored buildings that harken back to a bygone era.

Landmarks and Attractions:

The centerpiece of Portofino is its picturesque harbor, which is lined with luxury yachts, waterfront cafes, and upscale boutiques. Dominating the skyline is the iconic Church of San Giorgio, with its distinctive dome and bell tower standing as a symbol of the village's maritime heritage. Nearby, the Castello Brown offers panoramic views of the harbor and surrounding coastline, while the rugged cliffs of Paraggi Bay provide a stunning backdrop for sunbathing and swimming.

Activities and Excursions:

From leisurely strolls along the waterfront promenade to exhilarating boat trips to nearby coves and beaches, Portofino offers a wealth of activities for visitors to enjoy. Nature lovers can explore the scenic trails of the Portofino Regional Park, which winds through lush forests, rocky cliffs, and hidden coves, offering breathtaking views of the coastline and the Ligurian Sea. Adventurous souls can embark on diving expeditions to explore the underwater wonders of the Marine Protected Area, home to colorful coral reefs, marine life, and historic shipwrecks.

Dining and Cuisine:

Portofino's culinary scene is as diverse as it is delicious, with an abundance of seafood restaurants, trattorias, and gelaterias serving up fresh, flavorful dishes inspired by the region's coastal cuisine. From freshly caught fish and seafood pasta to creamy gelato and decadent pastries, there's something to satisfy every palate in this culinary paradise. Whether you're dining alfresco on the waterfront or enjoying a leisurely meal in a cozy trattoria, the flavors of Portofino are sure to leave a lasting impression.

Conclusion:

Portofino is a true gem of the Italian Riviera, a place where beauty, history, and luxury converge to create an unforgettable experience for visitors. Whether you're exploring its historic landmarks, soaking in the breathtaking views, or savoring the flavors of its cuisine, Portofino offers a slice of paradise that will leave you enchanted and longing to return. So pack your bags, set sail for the coast, and discover the magic of Portofino for yourself.

Cinque Terre: Exploring the Colorful Coastal Villages

Introduction:

Cinque Terre is a collection of five picturesque villages that have captured the hearts of travelers with their colorful houses, stunning cliffside views, and rich maritime heritage. Perched precariously on steep cliffs overlooking the Ligurian Sea, these charming villages offer visitors a glimpse into a simpler way of life, where time seems to stand still and the beauty of nature reigns supreme. In this chapter, we'll embark on a journey through Cinque Terre, exploring each village's unique charm, scenic landmarks, and the myriad of experiences that await those who venture to this coastal paradise.

Riomaggiore: A Painter's Palette:

The southernmost village of Cinque Terre, Riomaggiore, welcomes visitors with its vibrant colors, narrow alleyways, and bustling harbor. The village's iconic pastel-colored houses cling to the cliffsides like a cascade of rainbow hues, creating a picture-perfect backdrop for exploration. Highlights include the scenic waterfront promenade, the charming Church of San Giovanni Battista, and the medieval castle that overlooks the village, offering panoramic views of the coastline and the surrounding hills.

Manarola: A Seaside Spectacle:

Just a short walk from Riomaggiore lies Manarola, a postcard-perfect village perched on a rocky promontory overlooking the sea. With its colorful houses, terraced vineyards, and tranquil harbor, Manarola exudes a sense of serenity and charm that is quintessentially Cinque Terre. Visitors can stroll along the scenic Via dell'Amore, a romantic cliffside path that connects Manarola to Riomaggiore, or relax on the rocky beach and watch the sunset over the horizon.

Corniglia: A Hilltop Haven:

Located high above the sea on a rocky promontory, Corniglia offers visitors a tranquil retreat from the hustle and bustle of the coastal villages below. Surrounded by terraced vineyards and olive groves, the village boasts panoramic views of the surrounding countryside and the azure waters of the Mediterranean. Highlights include the medieval Church of San Pietro, the charming Piazza Largo Taragio, and the scenic hiking trails that wind through the nearby Cinque Terre National Park.

Vernazza: A Maritime Marvel:

Vernazza is perhaps the most iconic of the Cinque Terre villages, with its colorful houses clustered around a picturesque harbor and crowned by a medieval castle. Visitors can explore the winding streets and alleyways of the village, stopping to admire the historic Church of Santa Margherita d'Antiochia or enjoy a meal of fresh seafood at one of the waterfront trattorias. For the best views of Vernazza and the surrounding coastline, climb the steep steps to the top of the castle and marvel at the breathtaking panorama below.

Monterosso al Mare: A Beachfront Beauty:

The largest and most lively of the Cinque Terre villages, Monterosso al Mare is famous for its golden sandy beaches, crystal-clear waters, and vibrant seaside promenade. Visitors can relax on the beach, swim in the sea, or explore the charming old town, with its narrow streets, colorful houses, and lively piazzas. Highlights include the medieval Church of San Giovanni Battista, the historic Torre Aurora, and the bustling open-air market, where vendors sell fresh produce, seafood, and local specialties.

Conclusion:

Cinque Terre is a true coastal paradise, where the beauty of nature, the charm of the villages, and the warmth of the people combine to create an unforgettable experience for visitors. Whether you're exploring the colorful streets of Riomaggiore, hiking along the scenic trails of Corniglia, or soaking in the sun on the beaches of Monterosso al Mare, Cinque

Terre offers a wealth of experiences that will leave you enchanted and longing to return. So pack your bags, lace up your hiking boots, and discover the magic of Cinque Terre for yourself.

The Charm of Camogli and Santa Margherita Ligure

Introduction:

Camogli and Santa Margherita Ligure are two enchanting coastal towns that offer visitors a taste of traditional Italian seaside charm. With their colorful waterfronts, historic landmarks, and vibrant cultural scenes, these picturesque villages have long been favored destinations for travelers seeking relaxation, romance, and adventure. In this chapter, we'll delve into the allure of Camogli and Santa Margherita

Ligure, exploring their rich history, scenic landmarks, and the myriad of experiences that await those who venture to these coastal gems.

Camogli: A Seaside Sanctuary:

Known as the "City of the Thousand White Sails," Camogli is a postcard-perfect village nestled along the shores of the Ligurian Sea. With its colorful houses, bustling harbor, and tranquil beaches, Camogli exudes a sense of timeless charm and tranquility that has captivated visitors for generations. Highlights include the iconic Basilica of Santa Maria Assunta, with its distinctive dome and bell tower, the historic Castello della Dragonara, which offers panoramic views of the coastline, and the scenic Camogli promenade, where locals and visitors alike gather to soak in the sights and sounds of the sea.

Santa Margherita Ligure: A Riviera Retreat:

Just a short drive from Camogli lies Santa Margherita Ligure, a chic resort town renowned for its elegant architecture, pristine beaches, and vibrant cultural scene. The town's picturesque harbor is lined with luxury yachts, waterfront cafes, and upscale boutiques, while the historic center boasts charming piazzas, ornate villas, and lush gardens. Visitors can explore the stunning Villa Durazzo, with its terraced gardens and Baroque architecture, or relax on the sandy shores of Paraggi Beach, where the crystal-clear waters of the Mediterranean beckon swimmers and sunbathers alike.

Activities and Excursions:

From leisurely strolls along the waterfront promenades to exhilarating boat trips to nearby coves and beaches, Camogli and Santa Margherita Ligure offer a wealth of activities for visitors to enjoy. Nature lovers can explore the scenic hiking trails of the Portofino Regional Park, which wind through lush forests, rocky cliffs, and hidden coves, offering breathtaking views of the coastline and the Ligurian Sea. Adventurous souls can embark on diving expeditions to explore the underwater wonders of the Marine Protected Area, home to colorful coral reefs, marine life, and historic shipwrecks.

Dining and Cuisine:

Camogli and Santa Margherita Ligure are also renowned for their culinary delights, with an abundance of seafood restaurants, trattorias, and gelaterias serving up fresh, flavorful dishes inspired by the region's coastal cuisine. From freshly caught fish and seafood pasta to creamy gelato and decadent pastries, there's something to satisfy every palate in these coastal paradises. Whether you're dining alfresco on the waterfront or enjoying a leisurely meal in a cozy trattoria, the flavors of Camogli and Santa Margherita Ligure are sure to leave a lasting impression.

Conclusion:

Camogli and Santa Margherita Ligure are true jewels of the Italian Riviera, where beauty, history, and hospitality converge to create an unforgettable experience for visitors. Whether you're exploring the colorful streets of Camogli, soaking in the sun on the beaches of Santa Margherita Ligure, or indulging in the flavors of coastal cuisine, these charming villages offer a slice of paradise that will leave you enchanted and longing to return. So pack your bags, set sail for the coast, and discover the magic of Camogli and Santa Margherita Ligure for yourself.

Chapter Five: Practical Tips for a Seamless Genoa Experience

Accommodation Options: From Luxury Hotels to Cozy B&Bs

Introduction:

Choosing the perfect accommodation is a crucial part of any travel experience, and in Genoa, visitors are spoiled for choice with a diverse range of options to suit every taste and budget. From luxurious hotels with panoramic views of the sea to charming bed and breakfasts tucked away in historic neighborhoods, Genoa offers a wealth of accommodation options that cater to the needs and preferences of every traveler. In this chapter, we'll explore the different types of accommodation available in Genoa, highlighting their unique features, amenities, and the experiences they offer to guests.

Luxury Hotels:

For travelers seeking the ultimate in comfort, luxury, and indulgence, Genoa boasts a selection of five-star hotels that offer unparalleled service, exquisite amenities, and breathtaking views of the city and the sea. From historic palaces transformed into elegant hotels to sleek modern properties with state-of-the-art facilities, these luxury hotels cater to discerning guests who expect nothing but the best. With lavish suites, fine dining restaurants, spa facilities, and personalized concierge services, these hotels provide an unforgettable experience that epitomizes luxury living in Genoa.

Boutique Hotels:

For a more intimate and personalized experience, boutique hotels offer a charming alternative to the larger chain properties, with unique design, character, and style that reflect the spirit of Genoa. Housed in historic buildings and renovated palazzos, these boutique hotels offer a blend of old-world charm and modern amenities, with individually decorated rooms, cozy lounges, and personalized service that make guests feel right at home. Whether located in the heart of the historic center or overlooking the bustling port, boutique hotels offer a boutique experience that captures the essence of Genoa's rich cultural heritage.

Bed and Breakfasts (B&Bs):

For travelers seeking a more authentic and immersive experience, bed and breakfasts provide a cozy and welcoming alternative to traditional hotels. Run by friendly hosts who are eager to share their insider knowledge and recommendations, B&Bs offer a home-away-from-home atmosphere that fosters a sense of community and camaraderie among guests. With comfortable rooms, homemade breakfasts, and personalized service, B&Bs offer a relaxed and intimate retreat where guests can unwind, recharge, and connect with the local culture and lifestyle.

Vacation Rentals:

For those who prefer a more independent and flexible accommodation option, vacation rentals offer the freedom to create your own home base in Genoa. From stylish apartments in the historic center to seaside villas overlooking the Mediterranean, vacation rentals come in all shapes and sizes, catering to families, couples, and groups of friends alike. With fully equipped kitchens, spacious living areas, and private terraces or gardens, vacation rentals provide a comfortable and convenient option for travelers who want to experience life like a local in Genoa.

Conclusion:

Whether you're seeking a luxurious retreat, a charming boutique experience, a cozy bed and breakfast, or the flexibility of a vacation rental, Genoa offers a wealth of accommodation options to suit every taste and budget. With their unique charm, character, and hospitality, these accommodation options provide the perfect home base for exploring all that Genoa has to offer, ensuring that your stay in this captivating city is as comfortable, memorable, and enriching as possible. So choose your accommodation wisely, settle in, and prepare to embark on an unforgettable adventure in the charming city of Genoa.

Navigating Genoa's Transportation System

Introduction:

Navigating Genoa's transportation system is essential for any traveler looking to explore the city and its surrounding areas. With a network of buses, trains, ferries, and taxis, getting around Genoa is relatively straightforward, offering convenience and accessibility to visitors of all ages and interests. In this chapter, we'll delve into the various modes of transportation available in

Genoa, providing detailed information on routes, schedules, fares, and tips for making the most of your journey.

Public Transportation:

Genoa's public transportation system consists of buses and a metro line, providing reliable and efficient service to residents and visitors alike. The AMT (Azienda Mobilità e Trasporti) operates the city's bus network, with routes covering the entire metropolitan area and connecting major attractions, neighborhoods, and transportation hubs. The metro line, known as the Genoa Metro, offers a quick and convenient way to travel between the city center and outlying districts, with stations located at strategic points throughout the city.

Ferries and Water Taxis:

As a coastal city, Genoa offers the option of traveling by ferry or water taxi, providing scenic views of the harbor and the Ligurian Sea. The "Volabus" ferry service operates between the Old Port and other destinations along the coast, including Portofino, Camogli, and Santa Margherita Ligure, offering visitors a convenient way to explore the region's charming coastal villages. Water taxis are also available for private hire, providing a luxurious and personalized mode of transportation for those looking to travel in style.

Trains:

Genoa is well-connected to other cities and regions in Italy by train, with the Genoa Piazza Principe and Genoa Brignole railway stations serving as major transportation hubs. Trenitalia operates regional, intercity, and high-speed trains that connect Genoa to destinations such as Milan, Rome, Florence, and Venice, making it easy for travelers to explore the country's diverse landscapes, culture, and cuisine. The train stations are conveniently located in the city center, with easy access to public transportation and other amenities.

Taxis and Ride-Sharing Services:

Taxis are readily available in Genoa, providing a convenient option for travelers who prefer door-to-door service or need to reach destinations not served by public transportation. Taxis can be hailed on the street or booked in advance through the taxi companies' websites or mobile apps. In addition to traditional taxis, ride-sharing services such as Uber and Lyft are also available in Genoa, offering another option for getting around the city quickly and conveniently.

Renting a Car:

For travelers looking to explore the surrounding areas at their own pace, renting a car is a popular option in Genoa. Several car rental companies operate in the city, offering a wide range of vehicles to suit every budget and preference. With well-maintained roads and highways, driving in Genoa is relatively easy, although traffic congestion and limited parking can be a challenge in the city center. However, renting a car provides the flexibility to explore remote villages, scenic coastal drives, and hidden gems off the beaten path.

Conclusion:

Navigating Genoa's transportation system is a breeze with its diverse range of options, providing convenience, accessibility, and flexibility to travelers of all kinds. Whether you're exploring the city's historic landmarks, venturing to nearby coastal villages, or embarking on a scenic train journey through the Italian countryside, Genoa's transportation network ensures that you can reach your destination safely, efficiently, and comfortably. So plan your route, purchase your tickets, and embark on an unforgettable journey through the charming city of Genoa and beyond.

Insider Tips for Making the Most of Your Visit

Introduction:

Making the most of your visit to Genoa involves more than just visiting the main tourist attractions; it's about immersing yourself in the culture, history, and lifestyle of this vibrant city. From hidden gems and local favorites to practical advice and insider tips, this chapter is your guide to unlocking the true essence of Genoa and ensuring that your visit is memorable, authentic, and unforgettable.

Explore the Historic Center:

The heart of Genoa lies in its historic center, where narrow cobblestone streets wind their way through centuries-old buildings, bustling piazzas, and hidden courtyards. Take the time to wander off the beaten path and explore the charming alleyways and hidden corners of the old town, where you'll discover local shops, traditional trattorias, and artisan workshops that offer a glimpse into everyday life in Genoa.

Sample the Local Cuisine:

No visit to Genoa is complete without indulging in the city's culinary delights, from freshly caught seafood and savory street food to regional specialties like pesto and focaccia. Be sure to venture beyond the tourist areas and seek out authentic trattorias, osterias, and street vendors where locals gather to enjoy traditional Ligurian cuisine. Don't be afraid to try something new and ask for recommendations from locals, who are always eager to share their favorite spots.

Visit Off-the-Beaten-Path Attractions:
While Genoa's main attractions are certainly worth a visit, don't overlook the city's lesser-known gems and hidden treasures. Explore the quiet neighborhoods of Castelletto and Carignano, where you'll find panoramic viewpoints, historic villas, and charming parks that offer respite from the hustle and

bustle of the city center. Visit lesser-known museums and cultural institutions, such as the Galata Maritime Museum and the Wolfsoniana, to gain a deeper understanding of Genoa's rich maritime history and cultural heritage.

Take Advantage of Free Activities:

Genoa offers a wealth of free activities and attractions that allow visitors to experience the city's culture and beauty without breaking the bank. Take a leisurely stroll along the waterfront promenade, explore the colorful street art in the San Martino district, or visit one of the city's many parks and gardens for a relaxing afternoon in nature. Attend free concerts, exhibitions, and cultural events that take place throughout the year, providing opportunities to immerse yourself in Genoa's vibrant arts scene and connect with the local community.

Plan Ahead and Stay Flexible:

While it's important to have a rough itinerary and plan ahead for your visit to Genoa, it's also essential to stay flexible and open to new experiences. Embrace the spontaneity of travel and be willing to deviate from your plans to explore unexpected opportunities and hidden gems that you encounter along the way. Keep an open mind, be prepared for the unexpected, and allow yourself to get lost in the magic of Genoa.

Conclusion:

By following these insider tips and embracing the spirit of adventure, you'll be well-equipped to make the most of your visit to Genoa and create memories that will last a lifetime. Whether you're exploring the historic center, sampling local cuisine, or venturing off the beaten path, Genoa offers a wealth of experiences and opportunities for discovery that are sure to leave you enchanted and longing to return. So pack your bags, lace up your walking shoes, and prepare for an unforgettable journey through the charming streets and hidden corners of Genoa.

Conclusion

Fond Farewell to Genoa: Reflecting on Your Experience

As your time in Genoa comes to an end, it's natural to feel a sense of bittersweet nostalgia for the vibrant city that has captured your heart and imagination. Reflecting on your experiences, memories, and encounters, you'll find that Genoa has left an indelible mark on your soul, enriching your life with its beauty, culture, and charm.

Embracing the Spirit of Genoa:
Throughout your journey, you've embraced the spirit of Genoa, immersing yourself in its rich history, culture, and lifestyle. From exploring the labyrinthine streets of the

historic center to savoring the flavors of traditional Ligurian cuisine, you've discovered the true essence of this captivating city and its people. You've wandered through centuries-old palaces, marveled at majestic cathedrals, and soaked in the sights and sounds of the bustling ports, gaining a deeper appreciation for Genoa's maritime heritage and cultural diversity.

Connecting with the Locals:

One of the highlights of your visit has been connecting with the locals, who have welcomed you with open arms and shared their stories, traditions, and customs. Whether chatting with merchants at the local markets, sipping espresso at a neighborhood café, or sharing a meal with newfound friends, you've experienced the warmth, hospitality, and generosity of the

Genoese people, forging connections that transcend language and borders.

Discovering Hidden Gems:

Beyond the main tourist attractions, you've ventured off the beaten path to discover Genoa's hidden gems and secret treasures. From panoramic viewpoints and hidden gardens to tucked-away trattorias and artisan workshops, you've uncovered the city's hidden corners and lesser-known wonders, gaining a deeper understanding of its unique character and charm. You've embraced the spirit of exploration, curiosity, and adventure, allowing yourself to get lost in the maze of streets and alleyways, knowing that every turn reveals a new discovery and a new story to tell.

Leaving with Memories and Souvenirs:

As you bid farewell to Genoa, you carry with you not only memories of your time spent in this enchanting city but also souvenirs of the experiences, friendships, and moments that have touched your heart. Whether it's a piece of local artwork, a jar of homemade pesto, or a handwritten note from a newfound friend, these mementos serve as reminders of the magic of Genoa and the connections you've made along the way.

Looking Ahead with Gratitude and Anticipation:

As you depart Genoa and continue on your journey, you do so with gratitude for the experiences you've had, the lessons you've learned, and the memories you've created. You leave with a sense of anticipation for the adventures that lie ahead, knowing that the spirit of Genoa will continue to inspire and guide you wherever you go. Whether you return to Genoa someday or carry its spirit with you in your heart, you know that your fond farewell is not goodbye but rather "arrivederci"—until we meet again.

Conclusion:

Farewell, Genoa, with your winding streets and vibrant piazzas, your rich history and cultural heritage, your warm hospitality and timeless charm. As we bid adieu to this captivating city, we do so with a sense of gratitude, appreciation, and fondness for the experiences we've shared and the memories we've made. Until we meet again, may the spirit of Genoa live on in our hearts, guiding us on our journey and reminding us of the beauty and magic of this extraordinary place. Grazie mille, Genova, for an unforgettable experience—we'll carry you with us wherever we go. Arrivederci

Continuing Your Italian Adventures: Recommendations for Further Exploration

As your time in Genoa draws to a close, your journey through Italy is far from over. With its rich tapestry of culture, history, and natural beauty, Italy beckons travelers to explore its diverse regions, uncover hidden gems, and embark on new adventures. Whether you're drawn to the romantic canals of Venice, the ancient ruins of Rome, or the picturesque landscapes of Tuscany, there's no shortage of destinations to discover and experiences to savor. In this conclusion, we offer recommendations for further exploration, inspiring you to continue your Italian adventures beyond Genoa.

1. Venice: The City of Canals and Romance

No visit to Italy would be complete without experiencing the timeless beauty and romance of Venice. Wander through narrow alleyways, cross iconic bridges, and glide along picturesque canals in a traditional gondola, soaking in the enchanting atmosphere of this magical city. Explore world-class museums, admire stunning architecture, and savor authentic Venetian cuisine in charming trattorias and bacari. Venice is a feast for the senses and a must-visit destination for travelers seeking a truly unforgettable experience.

2. Rome: The Eternal City of History and Heritage

Step back in time and immerse yourself in the rich history and heritage of Rome, the

Eternal City. Marvel at iconic landmarks such as the Colosseum, the Roman Forum, and the Pantheon, which bear witness to millennia of civilization and culture. Explore the Vatican City, home to St. Peter's Basilica and the Sistine Chapel, and discover masterpieces of art and architecture that rival any in the world. Rome's bustling piazzas, lively markets, and vibrant neighborhoods offer endless opportunities for exploration and discovery, making it a must-see destination for history buffs, art enthusiasts, and culture lovers alike.

3. Florence: The Cradle of the Renaissance

Journey to the heart of Tuscany and discover the beauty and splendor of Florence, the Cradle of the Renaissance.

Admire world-famous artworks by Michelangelo, Leonardo da Vinci, and Botticelli at the Uffizi Gallery, marvel at the majestic Duomo and the Ponte Vecchio, and wander through historic streets lined with Renaissance palaces and gardens. Explore the Tuscan countryside, visit charming hilltop towns and vineyards, and savor the flavors of authentic Tuscan cuisine and wine. Florence is a treasure trove of art, culturo, and history that promises to captivate and inspire visitors of all ages.

4. Cinque Terre: A Coastal Paradise

For those seeking sun, sea, and spectacular scenery, the Cinque Terre is a must-visit destination. Explore the colorful coastal villages of Monterosso al Mare, Vernazza, Corniglia, Manarola, and Riomaggiore, each with its own unique charm and character. Hike along scenic trails that wind through terraced vineyards, olive groves, and rugged cliffs, offering breathtaking views of the Mediterranean Sea. Indulge in fresh seafood, swim in crystal-clear waters, and immerse yourself in the laid-back atmosphere of this coastal paradise. Cinque Terre is a haven for nature lovers, outdoor enthusiasts, and anyone seeking a tranquil escape from the hustle and bustle of everyday life.

5. Amalfi Coast: A Journey of Coastal Splendor

Embark on a journey along the Amalfi Coast, where dramatic cliffs, charming villages, and azure waters combine to create one of Italy's most breathtaking landscapes. Explore the picturesque towns of Positano, Amalfi, and

Ravello, each with its own unique allure and attractions. Drive along the winding coastal road, stopping to admire panoramic views, visit historic landmarks, and indulge in delicious local cuisine. Relax on sandy beaches, swim in hidden coves, and soak in the Mediterranean sun as you savor the beauty and tranquility of this stunning coastline.

Conclusion:

As you bid farewell to Genoa and continue your Italian adventures, may these recommendations inspire you to explore new destinations, discover hidden treasures, and create unforgettable memories along the way. Whether you choose to wander through the canals of Venice, marvel at the ancient ruins of Rome, or relax on the sun-drenched beaches of the Amalfi Coast, Italy promises endless opportunities for exploration, discovery, and adventure. So pack your bags, set sail for new horizons, and let the magic of Italy guide you on your journey. Buon viaggio.

Travel Planner

Destination (s)	When

Expenses	Budget	Actual

Transport ation		
Hotel		
Food		
Shopping		
Gifts		

Total		

Places to see

- _____

- _____

- _____

- _____

Places to eat

- _____

- _____

- _____

- _____

- _____

Places to shop

- _____

- _____

- _____

- _____

- _____

Emergency contacts

- _____

- _____

- _____

- _____

- _____

Addresses of places I'm staying at

- _____

- _____

- _____

- _____